date

from

to

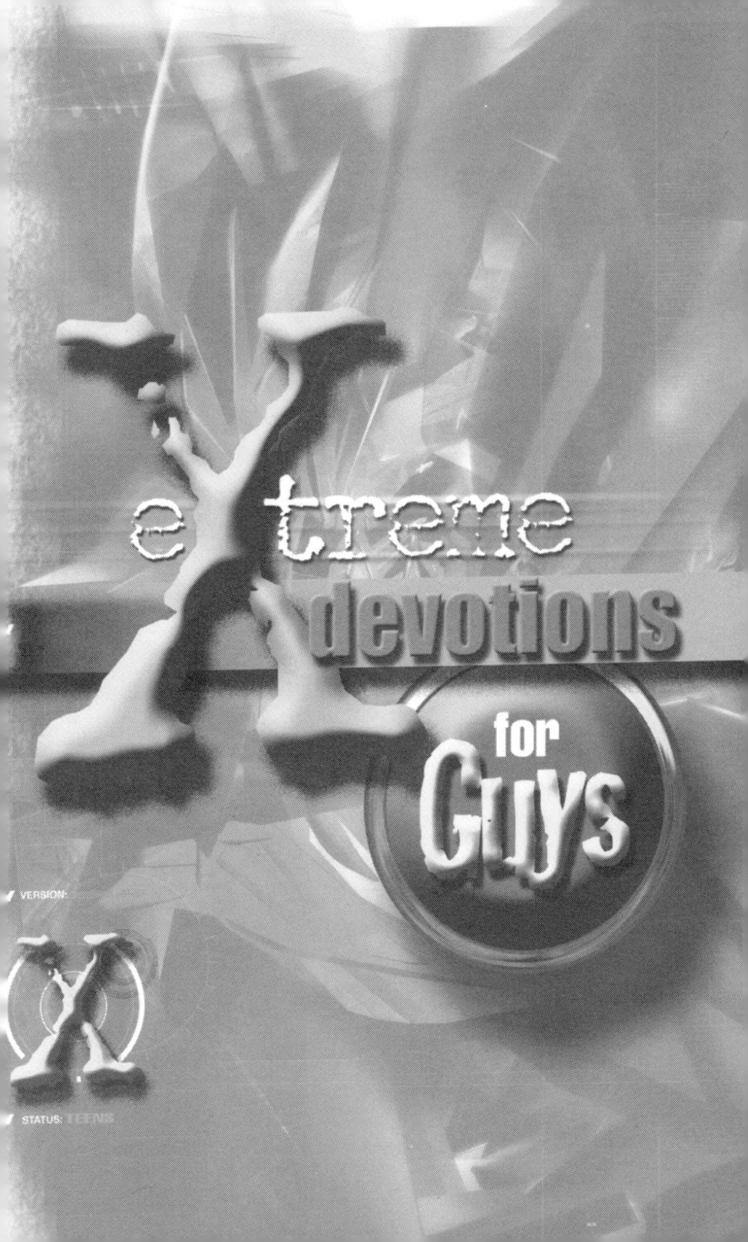

extreme
devotions
for Guys
VERSION:
STATUS: TEENS

Copyright ©2004 Walnut Grove Press
All rights reserved. No part of this book may be reproduced, stored in a retrieval system, or transmitted in any form or by any means—electronic, mechanical, photocopying, recording, or any other—except for brief quotations in printed reviews, without prior written permission of the publisher.

WALNUT GROVE PRESS
Nashville, TN 37202

The quoted ideas expressed in this book (but not scripture verses) are not, in all cases, exact quotations, as some have been edited for clarity and brevity. In all cases, the author has attempted to maintain the speaker's original intent. In some cases, quoted material for this book was obtained from secondary sources, primarily print media. While every effort was made to ensure the accuracy of these sources, the accuracy cannot be guaranteed. For additions, deletions, corrections or clarifications in future editions of this text, please write WALNUT GROVE PRESS.

Scripture quotations are taken from:

The Holy Bible, King James Version

The Holy Bible, New International Version (NIV) Copyright © 1973, 1978, 1984, by International Bible Society. Used by permission of Zondervan Publishing House. All rights reserved.

The New American Standard Bible®, (NASB) Copyright © 1960, 1962, 1963, 1968, 1971, 1972, 1973, 1975, 1977, 1995 by The Lockman Foundation. Used by permission.

The Holy Bible, New King James Version (NKJV) Copyright © 1982 by Thomas Nelson, Inc. Used by permission.

The Holy Bible, New Living Translation, (NLT) Copyright © 1996. Used by permission of Tyndale House Publishers, Inc., Wheaton, Illinois 60189. All rights reserved.

New Century Version®. (NCV) Copyright © 1987, 1988, 1991 by Word Publishing, a division of Thomas Nelson, Inc. All rights reserved. Used by permission.

The Message (MSG) This edition issued by contractual arrangement with NavPress, a division of The Navigators, U.S.A. Originally published by NavPress in English as THE MESSAGE: The Bible in Contemporary Language copyright 2002-2003 by Eugene Peterson. All rights reserved.

International Children's Bible®, New Century Version®. (ICB) Copyright © 1986, 1988, 1999 by Tommy Nelson™, a division of Thomas Nelson, Inc. All rights reserved. Used by permission.

The Holman Christian Standard Bible™ (HCSB) Copyright © 1999, 2000, 2001 by Holman Bible Publishers. Used by permission.

Cover Design by Kim Russell / Wahoo Designs
Page Layout by Bart Dawson

ISBN 1-58334-253-2

Printed in the United States of America

teens

e xtreme devotions

for Guys

Contents

Introduction

Face the facts: there was nothing middle-of-the-road about Jesus—He was extreme. He came to earth in an extremely unusual way. He made extreme claims; He did extreme things. And, He asked His followers to make extreme changes in their lives.

Now, here's the big question: Has Jesus made an extreme difference in *your* life, or are you satisfied to be a lukewarm believer who keeps Jesus at a "safe" distance? If you're determined to be a halfhearted Christian, then the idea of an extreme Jesus is probably a little bit unsettling, but if you desire to experience a more meaningful relationship with the One from Galilee, then the idea of following an extreme Jesus isn't very frightening at all.

This book can help you think about the extreme changes that Christ can—and should—make in your life. The text contains 31 devotional readings of particular interest to guys like you, guys who genuinely want to follow in the footsteps of Jesus. Each chapter contains Bible verses, a brief devotional

reading, quotations from noted thinkers, and a prayer.

Are you willing to make radical sacrifices for Jesus? If so, you may be certain of this fact: He's standing at the door of your heart, patiently waiting to form an extreme, life-altering relationship with you.

1

How Extreme Are You?

Don't look for shortcuts to God.
The market is flooded with surefire, easygoing formulas
for a successful life that can be practiced in
your spare time. Don't fall for that stuff,
even though crowds of people do.
The way to life—to God!—is vigorous and
requires total attention.

Matthew 7:13-14 MSG

Jesus made an extreme sacrifice for you. Are you willing to make extreme changes in your life for Him? Can you honestly say that you're passionate about your faith and that you're really following Jesus? Hopefully so. But if you're preoccupied with other things—or if you're strictly a one-day-a-week Christian—then you're in need of an extreme spiritual makeover!

Jesus doesn't want you to be a run-of-the-mill, follow-the-crowd kind of guy. Jesus wants you to be a "new creation" through Him. And that's exactly what you should want for yourself, too. Nothing is more important than your wholehearted commitment to your Creator and to His only begotten Son. Your faith must never be an afterthought; it must be your ultimate priority, your ultimate possession, and your ultimate passion.

You are the recipient of Christ's love. Accept it enthusiastically and share it passionately. Jesus deserves your extreme enthusiasm; the world deserves it; and you deserve the experience of sharing it.

How Extreme Are You?

When we realize and embrace the Lord's will for us,
we will love to do it.
We won't want to do anything else. It's a passion.

Franklin Graham

Today God's eyes are still running all across America . . .
the world . . . looking for someone, anyone,
who will totally and passionately seek him,
who is determined that every thought and action
will be pleasing in his sight. For such a person
or group, God will prove himself mighty.
His power will explode on their behalf.

Jim Cymbala

an eXtremely good idea

Be enthusiastic about your faith: John Wesley wrote, "You don't have to advertise a fire. Get on fire for God and the world will come to watch you burn." When you allow yourself to become extremely enthusiastic about your faith, other people will notice—and so will God.

If you do not stand firm in your faith,
you will not stand at all.

Isaiah 7:9 NIV

Lord, I give myself to you; my God, I trust you.

Psalm 25:1-2 NCV

Heavenly Father, thank You for
the gift of Your Son Jesus. I will be
His faithful, obedient servant, and I will make
fundamental changes in my life for Him.
I will be a passionate believer,
and I will praise You for Your blessings,
for Your love, and for Your Son.
Amen

2

Extreme
Faith

*But without faith it is impossible to please Him,
for he who comes to God must believe that He is,
and that He is a rewarder of those
who diligently seek Him.*

Hebrews 11:6 NKJV

Because we live in a demanding world, all of us have mountains to climb and mountains to move. Moving those mountains requires faith.

Are you a mountain-moving guy whose faith is evident for all to see? Or, are you a spiritual underachiever? As you think about the answer to that question, consider this: God needs more people who are willing to move mountains for His glory and for His kingdom.

Every life—including yours—is a series of wins and losses. Every step of the way, through every triumph and tragedy, God walks with you, ready and willing to strengthen you. So the next time you find your courage tested to the limit, remember to take your fears to God. If you call upon Him, you will be comforted. Whatever your challenge, whatever your trouble, God can handle it.

When you place your faith, your trust, indeed your life in the hands of your Heavenly Father, you'll be amazed at the marvelous things He can do with you and through you. So strengthen your faith through praise, through worship, through Bible study, and through prayer. And trust God's plans. With Him, all

Extreme Faith

things are possible, and He stands ready to open a world of possibilities to you . . . *if* you have faith.

And now, with no more delays, let the mountain moving begin.

Only God can move mountains,
but faith and prayer can move God.
E. M. Bounds

Following God will require faith and action.
Without faith you will not be able to please God.
When you act in faith, God is pleased.
Henry Blackaby and Claude King

an eXtremely good idea

Faith should be practiced more than studied.
Vance Havner said, "Nothing is more disastrous than to study faith, analyze faith, make noble resolves of faith, but never actually to make the leap of faith." How true!

*Yet faith comes from listening to this message
of good news—the Good News about Christ.*
Romans 10:17 NLT

*For in it the righteousness of God is revealed
from faith to faith; as it is written,
"The just shall live by faith."*
Romans 1:17 NKJV

Dear Lord, guide me away from
the temptations and distractions of
this world, and make me a champion of
the faith. Today I will honor You
with my thoughts, my actions,
and my prayers. I will worship You, Father,
with gratitude in my heart
and praise on my lips, this day and forever.
Amen

3

Extreme Wisdom

Those who are wise will shine like the brightness of the heavens, and those who lead many to righteousness, like the stars forever and ever.

Daniel 12:3 NIV

Are you a wise guy? Hopefully, you're a very wise fellow who's getting wiser every day. But even if you're a very smart fellow, there's still lots more for you to learn.

Wisdom is not like a dandelion or a mushroom; it does not spring up overnight. It is, instead, like an oak tree that starts as a tiny acorn, grows into a sapling, and eventually reaches up to the sky, tall and strong. To become wise, you must seek God's wisdom and live according to His Word. To become wise, you must seek wisdom with consistency and purpose. To become wise, you must not only *learn* the lessons of the Christian life, you must also *live* by them.

Are you passionate in your pursuit of God's wisdom? And do you sincerely seek to live a life of righteousness? If so, you must study the ultimate source of wisdom: the Word of God. You must seek out worthy teachers and listen carefully to their advice. You must associate, day in and day out, with godly friends. And, you must act in accordance with your beliefs. When you do these things, you will become wise . . . and you will be a blessing to your friends, to your family, and to the world.

Extreme Wisdom

God does not give His counsel to the curious
or the careless; He reveals His will to the concerned
and to the consecrated.

Warren Wiersbe

Don't expect wisdom to come into your life like
great chunks of rock on a conveyor belt.
Wisdom comes privately from God as a byproduct
of right decisions, godly reactions, and the application
of spiritual principles to daily circumstances.

Charles Swindoll

There are some things that can be learned by the head,
but Christ crucified can only be learned by the heart.

C. H. Spurgeon

an eXtremely good idea

Wisdom 101: If you're looking for wisdom, the Book of Proverbs is a wonderful place to start. It has 31 chapters, one for each day of the month. If you read Proverbs regularly, and if you take its teachings to heart, you'll gain timeless wisdom from God's unchanging Word.

*But if any of you needs wisdom,
you should ask God for it. He is generous
and enjoys giving to all people,
so he will give you wisdom.*

James 1:5 NCV

He who walks with the wise grows wise . . . .

Proverbs 13:20 NIV

Dear Lord, when I depend upon
the world's wisdom, I make many mistakes.
But when I trust in Your wisdom,
I build my life on a firm foundation.
Today and every day I will trust Your Word
and follow it, knowing that the ultimate
wisdom is Your wisdom and
the ultimate truth is Your truth.

Amen

4

God Has a Plan... Are You Interested?

The LORD will work out his plans for my life—
for your faithful love, O LORD, endures forever.

Psalm 138:8 NLT

Do you think that God has big plans for you, or do think that God wants you to be a do-nothing Christian? The answer should be obvious, but just for the record, here are the facts:

1. God has plans for your life that are far grander than you can imagine.

2. It's up to you to discover those plans and accomplish them . . . or not.

God has given you many gifts, including the gift of free will; that means that you have the ability to make choices and decisions on your own. The most important decision of your life is, of course, your commitment to accept Jesus Christ as your personal Lord and Savior. And once your eternal destiny is secured, you will undoubtedly ask yourself, "What now, Lord?" If you earnestly seek God's plan for your life, you will find it . . . in time.

Sometimes, God's plans are crystal clear, but other times, He may lead you through the wilderness before He delivers you to the Promised Land. So be patient, keep praying, and keep seeking His will for your life. When you do, you'll be amazed at the marvelous things that an all-powerful, all-knowing God can do.

God Has a Plan . . . Are You Interested?

The one supreme business of life is to find
God's plan for your life and live it.
E. Stanley Jones

A saint's life is in the hands of God just as a bow
and arrow are in the hands of an archer.
God is aiming at something the saint cannot see.
Oswald Chambers

God will not permit any troubles to come upon us
unless He has a specific plan by which
great blessings can come out of the difficulty.
Peter Marshall

an eXtremely good idea

Your plans, or God's plans? As you plan for this day and for all the ones that follow it, you should do so in prayerful consultation with your Father in heaven. If you make plans that are outside of God's will, you will experience unwelcome consequences. A far better strategy is to consult God earnestly and consistently before you embark upon the next stage of your life's journey. Then, as you sense His intentions, follow them.

"I say this because I know what I am
planning for you," says the Lord.
"I have good plans for you, not plans to hurt you.
I will give you hope and a good future."

Jeremiah 29:11 NCV

Who are those who fear the LORD?
He will show them the path they should choose.
They will live in prosperity, and their children
will inherit the Promised Land.

Psalm 25:12-13 NLT

Dear Lord, let me choose Your plans.
You created me, and You have called me
to do Your work here on earth. Today,
I choose to seek Your will and to live it,
knowing that when I trust in You,
I am eternally blessed.
Amen

28

5

Extreme Forgiveness

*Then Peter came to him and asked,
"Lord, how often should I forgive someone
who sins against me? Seven times?"
"No!" Jesus replied, "seventy times seven!"*

Matthew 18:21-22 NLT

F orgiving other people is hard—sometimes *very* hard. But God tells us that we must forgive others, even when we'd rather not. So, if you're angry with anybody (or if you're upset by something you yourself have done) it's time to forgive . . . *now!*

Life would be much simpler if you could forgive people "once and for all" and be done with it. Yet forgiveness is seldom that easy. Usually, the *decision* to forgive is straightforward, but the *process* of forgiving is more difficult. Forgiveness is a journey that requires effort, time, perseverance, and prayer.

God instructs you to treat other people exactly as you wish to be treated. And since you want to be forgiven for the mistakes that you make, you must be willing to extend forgiveness to other people for the mistakes that they have made. If you can't seem to forgive someone, you should keep asking God to help you until you do. And you can be sure of this: if you keep asking for God's help, He will give it.

for Guys

The fire of anger, if not quenched by loving
forgiveness, will spread and defile
and destroy the work of God.

Warren Wiersbe

Two works of mercy set a man free:
forgive and you will be forgiven,
and give and you will receive.

St. Augustine

An eye for an eye and a tooth for a tooth . . .
and pretty soon, everybody's blind
and wearing false teeth.

Anonymous

an eXtremely good idea

What if it's really difficult to forgive somebody?
If forgiveness were easy, everybody would be doing
it—but it's not always easy to forgive and forget.
If you simply can't seem to forgive someone, start
praying about it . . . and keep praying about it . . .
until God helps you do the right thing.

*You have heard that it was said,
"Love your neighbor and hate your enemy."
But I tell you: Love your enemies
and pray for those who persecute you.*

Matthew 5:43-44 NIV

*If you forgive those who sin against you,
your heavenly Father will forgive you.
But if you refuse to forgive others,
your Father will not forgive your sins.*

Matthew 6:14-15 NLT

Heavenly Father, forgiveness is
Your commandment, and I know that I should
forgive others just as You have forgiven me.
But, genuine forgiveness is difficult.
Help me to forgive those who have injured me,
and deliver me from the traps of anger
and bitterness. Forgiveness is Your way,
Lord; let it be mine.
Amen

6

Your Priorities and God's ... How Similar Are They?

*The thing you should want most is God's kingdom
and doing what God wants.
Then all these other things you need
will be given to you.*

Matthew 6:33 NCV

Here's a quick quiz:

Whose expectations are you trying to meet?

A. Your friends' expectations
B. Society's expectations
C. God's expectations

If you're a Christian, the correct answer is C., but if you're overly concerned with either A or B, you're not alone. Plenty of guys invest too much energy trying to meet society's expectations and too little energy trying to please God. It's a common behavior, but it's also a very big mistake.

A better strategy, of course, is to try to please God first. To do so, you must prioritize your day according to God's commandments, and you must seek His will and His wisdom in all matters. Then, you can face each day with the assurance that the same God who created our universe out of nothingness will help you place first things first in your own life.

Are you having trouble choosing between God's priorities and society's priorities? Are you feeling overwhelmed or confused? If so, turn the concerns over to God—prayerfully, earnestly, and often. Then, listen for His answer . . . and trust the answer He gives.

Your Priorities and God's . . . How Similar Are They?

Whatever you love most, be it sports, pleasure,
business, or God, that is your god.

Billy Graham

Give me the person who says, "This one thing I do,
and not these fifty things I dabble in."

D. L. Moody

Don't take hold of a thing unless you want that thing
to take hold of you.

E. Stanley Jones

No test of a man's true character is more conclusive
than how he spends his time and his money.

Patrick Morley

an eXtremely good idea

Make God a priority: Your days are probably filled
to the brim with lots of obligations. But remember:
no obligation is greater than the debt you owe to
your Creator. So make sure that you give Him the
time He deserves, not only on Sundays but also on
every other day of the week.

He said to them all, "If anyone desires to come
after Me, let him deny himself, and take up
his cross daily, and follow Me. For whoever desires
to save his life will lose it, but whoever
loses his life for My sake will save it."

Luke 9:23-24 NKJV

Let us fix our eyes on Jesus, the author and perfecter
of our faith, who for the joy set before him endured
the cross, scorning its shame, and sat down
at the right hand of the throne of God.

Hebrews 12:2 NIV

Lord, let Your priorities be my priorities.
Let Your will be my will. Let Your Word be
my guide, and let me grow in faith
and in wisdom this day and every day.

Amen

for Guys

7

Extreme Temptation

*Then Jesus told him, "Go away, Satan!
For it is written: You must worship the Lord your God,
and you must serve Him only."*

Matthew 4:10 HCSB

We live in a world filled with an extreme number of temptations. The devil is working overtime causing pain and heartache in more places and in more ways than ever before. We, as followers of Christ, must remain vigilant. Not only must we resist Satan when he confronts us, but we must also avoid those places where Satan can most easily tempt us. And, if we are to avoid the unending temptations of this world, we must arm ourselves with the Word of God.

In a letter to believers, Peter offered a stern warning: "Your adversary, the devil, prowls around like a roaring lion, seeking someone to devour" (I Peter 5:8 NASB). What was true in New Testament times is equally true in our own. Satan tempts his prey and then devours them.

As believing Christians, we must be watchful and we must beware. And, if we seek righteousness in our own lives, we must earnestly wrap ourselves in the protection of God's Holy Word. When we do, we are protected.

Many times the greatest temptations confront us
when we are in the center of the will of God,
because being there has offset and frustrated
Satan's methods of attack.

Franklin Graham

In the worst temptations nothing can help us
but faith that God's Son has put on flesh,
sits at the right hand of the Father, and prays for us.
There is no mightier comfort.

Martin Luther

If you don't avoid the bait . . .
you'll end up on the hook.

Anonymous

an eXtremely good idea

Pray a little more: If life's inevitable temptations
seem to be getting the best of you, try praying
more often, even if many of those prayers are
simply brief, "open-eyed" requests to your Father
in heaven.

*For we do not have a high priest who is unable
to sympathize with our weaknesses, but we have
one who has been tempted in every way,
just as we are—yet was without sin.*

Hebrews 4:15 NIV

*The Lord knows how to deliver
the godly out of temptations.*

2 Peter 2:9 NKJV

Dear Lord, this world is filled with
temptations, distractions, and frustrations.
When I turn my thoughts away from You
and Your Word, Lord, I suffer bitter
consequences. But, when I trust in Your
commandments, I am safe. Direct my path
far from the temptations and distractions
of the world. Let me discover Your will and
follow it, Dear Lord, this day and always.
Amen

8

So Much to Do; So Little Time!

To every thing there is a season, and a time to every purpose under the heaven: A time to be born, and a time to die; a time to plant, and a time to pluck up that which is planted; A time to kill, and a time to heal; a time to break down, and a time to build up; A time to weep, and a time to laugh; a time to mourn, and a time to dance; . . . a time to keep silence, and a time to speak; A time to love, and a time to hate; a time of war, and a time of peace.

Ecclesiastes 3:1-8 KJV

Time is a nonrenewable gift from God. But sometimes, we treat our time here on earth as if it were not a gift at all: We may be tempted to invest our lives in trivial pursuits and petty diversions. But our Father beckons each of us to a higher calling.

An important element of our stewardship to God is the way that we choose to spend the time He has entrusted to us. Each waking moment holds the potential to hug a child or do a good deed or say a kind word or to offer a heartfelt prayer. Our challenge, as believers, is to use our time wisely in the service of God's work and in accordance with His plan for our lives.

Today, like every day, is a special treasure to be savored and celebrated. May we—as Christians who have so much to celebrate—never fail to praise our Creator by rejoicing in this glorious day . . . and by using it wisely.

Our leisure, even our play, is a matter of
serious concern. There is no neutral ground in
the universe: every square inch, every split second,
is claimed by God and counterclaimed by Satan.

C. S. Lewis

God has a present will for your life. It is neither
chaotic nor utterly exhausting. In the midst of many
good choices vying for your time, He will give you
the discernment to recognize what is best.

Beth Moore

The best use of life is love.
The best expression of love is time.
The best time to love is now.

Rick Warren

an eXtremely good idea

Today is a cause for celebration: Psalm 118:24
has clear instructions for the coming day: "This is
the day which the LORD has made; let us rejoice
and be glad in it." Plan your day—and your
life—accordingly.

*So teach us to number our days,
that we may gain a heart of wisdom.*

Psalm 90:12 NKJV

*Lord, tell me when the end will come and how long
I will live. Let me know how long I have.
You have given me only a short life;
my lifetime is like nothing to you.
Everyone's life is only a breath.*

Psalm 39:4-5 NCV

Dear Lord, You have given me
a wonderful gift: time here on earth.
Let me use it wisely today
and every day that I live.
Amen

Peer Pressure: Positive or Negative?

Blessed is the man who walks not in the counsel of the ungodly, nor stands in the path of sinners, nor sits in the seat of the scornful; but his delight is in the law of the LORD, and in His law he meditates day and night.

Psalm 1:1-2 NKJV

Our world is filled with pressures: some good, some bad. The pressures that we feel to follow God's will and to obey His commandments are positive pressures. God places them on our hearts, and He intends that we act in accordance with these feelings. But we also face different pressures, ones that are definitely *not* from God. When we feel pressured to do things—or even to think thoughts—that lead us away from God, we must beware.

Rick Warren observed, "Those who follow the crowd usually get lost in it." We know these words to be true, but oftentimes we fail to live by them. Instead of trusting God for guidance, we imitate our friends and suffer the consequences. Instead of seeking to please our Father in heaven, we strive to please our peers, with decidedly mixed results. Instead of doing the right thing, we do the "easy" thing or the "popular" thing. And when we do, we pay a high price for our shortsightedness.

Are you satisfied to follow the crowd, or will you follow the One from Galilee? If you sincerely want to please God, you must resist the pressures that society seeks to impose upon you, and you must conform yourself, instead, to God's will, to His path, and to His Son.

Peer Pressure: Positive or Negative?

> Fashion is an enduring testimony
> to the fact that we live quite consciously
> before the eyes of others.
>
> *John Eldredge*

> If you try to be everything to everybody,
> you will end up being nothing to anybody.
>
> *Vance Havner*

an eXtremely good idea

Peer Pressure 101: Here's what you need to know about peer pressure:

1. Peer pressure exists, and you will experience it.
2. If your peers encourage you to behave yourself, to honor God, and to become a better person, peer pressure can actually be a good thing . . . up to a point. But remember: you don't have to be perfect to be wonderful. So if you're trying to be perfect, lighten up on yourself, and while you're at it, lighten up on others, too. If your friends are encouraging you to misbehave or underachieve, find new friends. Today. End of lecture.

Stay away from a foolish man,
for you will not find knowledge on his lips.

Proverbs 14:7 NIV

Obviously, I'm not trying to be a people pleaser!
No, I am trying to please God.
If I were still trying to please people,
I would not be Christ's servant.

Galatians 1:10 NLT

Dear Lord, today I will worry less about pleasing other people and more about pleasing You. I will stand up for my beliefs, and I will honor You with my thoughts, my actions, and my prayers. And I will worship You, Father, with thanksgiving in my heart, this day and forever.

Amen

Too Much Stuff . . .

Keep your lives free from the love of money,
and be satisfied with what you have.

Hebrews 13:5 NCV

"So much stuff to shop for, and so little time . . ." These words seem to describe the priorities of our 21st-century world. Hopefully, you're not building your life around your next visit to the local mall—but you can be sure that many people are!

Our society is in love with money and the things that money can buy. God is not. God cares about people, not possessions, and so must we. We must, to the best of our abilities, love our neighbors as ourselves, and we must, to the best of our abilities, resist the mighty temptation to place possessions ahead of people.

Money, in and of itself, is not evil; worshipping money is. So today, as you prioritize matters of importance for you and yours, remember that God is almighty, but the dollar is not.

If we worship God, we are blessed. But if we worship "the almighty dollar," we are inevitably punished because of our misplaced priorities—and our punishment inevitably comes sooner rather than later.

If you want to be truly happy, you won't find it
on an endless quest for more stuff. You'll find it
in receiving God's generosity and in passing
that generosity along.

Bill Hybels

When possessions become our god, we become
materialistic and greedy . . . and we forfeit
our contentment and our joy.

Charles Swindoll

We act as though comfort and luxury were
the chief requirements of life, when all we need
to make us really happy is something to
be enthusiastic about.

Charles Kingsley

He is no fool who gives what he cannot keep
to gain what he cannot lose.

Jim Elliot

an eXtremely good idea

Stuff 101: The world says, "Buy more stuff." God
says, "Stuff isn't important." Believe God.

We brought nothing into the world,
so we can take nothing out.
But, if we have food and clothes,
we will be satisfied with that.
1 Timothy 6:7-8 NCV

Then Jesus said to them,
"Be careful and guard against all kinds of greed.
Life is not measured by how much one owns."
Luke 12:15 NCV

Lord, my greatest possession is
my relationship with You through
Jesus Christ. You have promised that,
when I first seek Your kingdom and
Your righteousness, You will give me
whatever I need. Let me trust You completely,
Lord, for my needs, both material and
spiritual, this day and always.
Amen

Extreme Patience

*So don't lose a minute in building on what
you've been given, complementing your basic faith
with good character, spiritual understanding,
alert discipline, passionate patience, reverent wonder,
warm friendliness, and generous love, each dimension
fitting into and developing the others.*

2 Peter 1:5-7 MSG

A re you an extremely patient guy? If so, feel free to skip the rest of this page. But if you're not, here's something to think about: If you really want to become a more patient person, God is ready and willing to help.

The Bible promises that when you sincerely seek God's help, He will give you the things that you need—and that includes patience. But God won't force you to become a more patient person. If you want to become a more mature Christian, you've got to do some of the work yourself—and the best time to start doing that work is now.

So, if you want to gain patience and maturity, bow your head and start praying about it. Then, rest assured that with God's help you can most certainly make yourself a more patient, understanding, and mature Christian.

Patience is the companion of wisdom.
St. Augustine

God freely admits he is holding back his power,
but he restrains himself for our benefit.
For all scoffers who call for direct action from
the heavens, the prophets have ominous advice:
Just wait.
Philip Yancey

Teach us, O Lord, the disciplines of patience,
for to wait is often harder than to work.
Peter Marshall

an eXtremely good idea

**The best things in life seldom happen overnight
. . . they usually take time:** Henry Blackaby writes,
"The grass that is here today and gone tomorrow
does not require much time to mature. A big oak
tree that lasts for generations requires much more
time to grow and mature. God is concerned about
your life through eternity. Allow Him to take all
the time He needs to shape you for His purposes.
Larger assignments will require longer periods of
preparation." How true!

Always be humble, gentle, and patient,
accepting each other in love.

Ephesians 4:2 NCV

Patience is better than strength.

Proverbs 16:32 NCV

Yet the LORD longs to be gracious to you;
he rises to show you compassion.
For the LORD is a God of justice.
Blessed are all who wait for him!

Isaiah 30:18 NIV

Lord, sometimes I am not very patient.
Slow me down and calm me down.
Help me to think wisely and to act wisely.
Today and every day, help me to learn
the wisdom of patience.

Amen

for Guys

12

Extreme Gratitude

*Everything created by God is good,
and nothing is to be rejected,
if it is received with gratitude;
for it is sanctified by means of
the word of God and prayer.*

I Timothy 4:4-5 NASB

I f you're like most guys on the planet, you're a very busy fellow. Your life is probably hectic, demanding, and complicated. When the demands of life leave you rushing from place to place with scarcely a moment to spare, you may fail to pause and thank your Creator for the blessings He has bestowed upon you. Big mistake.

No matter how busy you are, you should *never* be too busy to thank God for His gifts. Your task, as an extreme follower of the living Christ, is to praise God many times each day. After all, your Heavenly Father has blessed you beyond measure, and you owe Him everything, including your thanks, starting now.

> Thanksgiving is good but Thanksliving is better.
>
> *Jim Gallery*

My "think tank" may be runnin' on empty,
but, praise the Lord, my "thank tank" is full.
Marie T. Freeman

Think of the blessings we so easily take for granted:
Life itself; preservation from danger;
every bit of health we enjoy; every hour of liberty;
the ability to see, to hear, to speak, to think,
and to imagine all this comes from the hand of God.
Billy Graham

The words "thank" and "think"
come from the same root word.
If we would think more, we would thank more.
Warren Wiersbe

an eXtremely good idea

When is the best time to say "thanks" to God?
Anytime. God never takes a vacation, and He's
always ready to hear from you. So what are you
waiting for?

Be cheerful no matter what; pray all the time;
thank God no matter what happens.
This is the way God wants you
who belong to Christ Jesus to live.

1 Thessalonians 5:16-18 MSG

As you therefore have received Christ Jesus the Lord,
so walk in Him, having been firmly rooted
and now being built up in Him and established
in your faith, just as you were instructed,
and overflowing with gratitude.

Colossians 2:6-7 NASB

Lord, let my attitude be one of gratitude.
You have given me much; when I think of
Your grace and goodness, I am humbled
and thankful. Today, let me express my
thanksgiving, Father, not just through
my words but also through my deeds . . .
and may all the glory be Yours.
Amen

13

Sharing Your Faith

But when the Holy Spirit has come upon you,
you will receive power and will tell people
about me everywhere—in Jerusalem,
throughout Judea, in Samaria,
and to the ends of the earth.

Acts 1:8 NLT

Our personal testimonies are extremely important, but sometimes, because of shyness or insecurities, we're afraid to share our experiences. And that's unfortunate.

In his second letter to Timothy, Paul shares a message to believers of every generation when he writes, "God has not given us a spirit of timidity" (1:7). Paul's meaning is clear: When sharing our beliefs, we, as Christians, must be courageous, forthright, and unashamed.

We live in a world that desperately needs the healing message of Christ Jesus. Every believer, each in his or her own way, bears responsibility for sharing the Good News of our Savior.

Billy Graham observed, "Our faith grows by expression. If we want to keep our faith, we must share it." If you are a follower of Christ, the time to express your belief in Him is now. You know how He has touched your heart; help Him do the same for others.

To stand in an uncaring world and say,
"See, here is the Christ" is a daring act of courage.
Calvin Miller

Our Lord is searching for people who will
make a difference. Christians dare not dissolve
into the background or blend into
the neutral scenery of the world.
Charles Swindoll

Nothing else you do will ever matter
as much as helping people establish
an eternal relationship with God!
Rick Warren

an eXtremely good idea

Your story is important: D. L. Moody, the famed
evangelist from Chicago, said, "Remember, a small
light will do a great deal when it is in a very dark
place. Put one little tallow candle in the middle of
a large hall, and it will give a great deal of light."
It's up to you to make certain that your candle is
always lit. So give your testimony, and trust God
to do the rest.

Christ did not send me to baptize people
but to preach the Good News.
And he sent me to preach the Good News
without using words of human wisdom so that
the cross of Christ would not lose its power.

1 Corinthians 1:17 NCV

And I say to you, everyone who confesses Me
before men, the Son of Man will confess him
also before the angels of God . . . .

Luke 12:8 NASB

Dear Lord, You sent Your Son Jesus to die
on a cross for me. Jesus endured indignity,
suffering, and death so that I might live.
Because He lives, I, too, have Your promise
of eternal life. Let me share this Good News,
Lord, with a world that so desperately needs
Your healing hand and the salvation of
Your Son. Today, let me share the message
of Jesus Christ through my words
and my deeds.
Amen

14

Extreme Familiarity with Your Bible

There's nothing like the written Word of God for
showing you the way to salvation through faith in
Christ Jesus. Every part of Scripture is God-breathed
and useful one way or another, showing us truth,
exposing our rebellion, correcting our mistakes,
training us to live God's way. Through the Word
we are put together and shaped up for
the tasks God has for us.

2 Timothy 3:15-17 MSG

Do you read your Bible a lot . . . or not? The answer to this simple question will determine, to a surprising extent, the quality of your life *and* the direction of your faith.

As you establish priorities for life, you must decide whether God's Word will be a bright spotlight that guides your path every day or a tiny nightlight that occasionally flickers in the dark. The decision to study the Bible—or not—is yours and yours alone. But make no mistake: how you choose to use your Bible will have a profound impact on you and your loved ones.

The Bible is unlike any other book. It is a priceless gift from your Creator, a tool that God intends for you to use in every aspect of your life. And, it contains promises upon which you, as a Christian, can and must depend.

Jonathan Edwards advised, "Be assiduous in reading the Holy Scriptures. This is the fountain whence all knowledge in divinity must be derived. Therefore let not this treasure lie by you neglected."

God's Holy Word is, indeed, a priceless, one-of-a-kind treasure. Handle it with care, but, more importantly, handle it every day.

> Nobody ever outgrows Scripture; the book widens
> and deepens with our years.
>
> *C. H. Spurgeon*

> I study the Bible as I gather apples.
> First, I shake the whole tree that the ripest might fall.
> Then I shake each limb; I shake each branch
> and every twig. Then, I look under every leaf.
>
> *Martin Luther*

> Some read the Bible to learn,
> and some read the Bible to hear from heaven.
>
> *Andrew Murray*

an eXtremely good idea

The Bible is the best-selling book of all time . . . for good reason. Ruth Bell Graham, wife of evangelist Billy Graham, believes in the importance of God's Word: "The Reference Point for the Christian is the Bible. All values, judgments, and attitudes must be gauged in relationship to this Reference Point." Make certain that you're an avid reader of God's best-seller, and make sure that you keep reading it as long as you live!

Man shall not live by bread alone,
but by every word that proceeds
from the mouth of God.

Matthew 4:4 NKJV

For I am not ashamed of the gospel of Christ,
for it is the power of God to salvation
for everyone who believes.

Romans 1:16 NKJV

Lord, You've given me instructions for
life here on earth and for life eternal.
I will use the Bible as my guide. I will study it
and meditate upon it as I trust You, Lord,
to speak to me through Your Holy Word.
Amen

15

Extreme
Discipline

*But I discipline my body and bring it into subjection,
lest, when I have preached to others,
I myself should become disqualified.*

I Corinthians 9:27 NKJV

Are you a self-disciplined guy? If so, congratulations . . . if not, God wants to have a little talk with you.

God doesn't reward laziness, misbehavior, or apathy. To the contrary, He expects His followers to behave with dignity and discipline. But sometimes, it's extremely difficult to be dignified and disciplined. Why? Because the world wants us to believe that dignified, self-disciplined behavior is going out of style.

You live in a world in which leisure is glorified and indifference is often glamorized. But God has other plans. He did not create you to be ordinary; He created you for far greater things.

Face facts: Life's greatest rewards aren't likely to fall into your lap. To the contrary, your greatest accomplishments will probably require lots of work, which is perfectly fine with God. After all, He knows that you're up to the task, and He has big plans for you. God will do His part to fulfill those plans, and the rest, of course, is up to you.

Now, are you steadfast in your determination to be a self-disciplined guy? If so, congratulations . . . if not, reread this little essay—and keep reading it—until God's message finally sinks in.

If one examines the secret behind a championship
football team, a magnificent orchestra,
or a successful business, the principal ingredient
is invariably discipline.

James Dobson

The goal of any discipline is to result
in greater freedom.

Anonymous

The effective Christians of history have been men
and women of great personal discipline—
mental discipline, discipline of the body,
discipline of the tongue, and discipline of the emotion.

Billy Graham

an eXtremely good idea

Discipline is not a four-letter word: Exercising
discipline should never be viewed as an imposition
or as a form of punishment; far from it. Discipline
is the means by which you can take control of your
life (which, by the way, is far better than letting
your life control you).

*Do you not know that those who run
in a race all run, but only one receives the prize?
Run in such a way that you may win.
Everyone who competes in the games
exercises self-control in all things.*
1 Corinthians 9:24-25 NASB

Discipline yourself for the purpose of godliness.
1 Timothy 4:7 NASB

Lord, I want to be a disciplined believer.
Let me use my time wisely, and let me
teach others by the faithfulness of
my conduct, today and every day.
Amen

16

Spiritual
Maturity
Day by Day

*Long for the pure milk of the word,
so that by it you may grow in respect to salvation.*

I Peter 2:2 *NASB*

hen will you be a "fully-grown" Christian man? Hopefully never—or at least not until you arrive in heaven! As a believer living here on planet earth, you're never "fully grown;" you always have the potential to keep growing.

As a Christian, you should continue to grow in the love and the knowledge of your Savior as long as you live. How? By studying God's Word, by obeying His commandments, and by allowing His Son to reign over your heart.

Are you seeking to become a more mature believer? Hopefully so, because that's exactly what God wants you to become . . . and it's exactly what you should want to become, too!

In those quiet moments when you open your heart to God, the One who made you keeps remaking you. He gives you direction day by day. So, give God a few minutes each morning. When you do, He will change the tone and direction of your life.

Every Christian would agree that a man's spiritual
health is exactly proportional to his love for God.
C. S. Lewis

I've never met anyone who became instantly mature.
It's a painstaking process that God takes us through,
and it includes such things as waiting, failing,
losing, and being misunderstood—
each calling for extra doses of perseverance.
Charles Swindoll

It is tempting to imagine that, given a different lot
in life, circumstances other than those in which we
find ourselves, we would make much greater strides
in holiness. The truth is that the place where
we are is God's schoolroom, not somewhere else.
Here we may be conformed to the likeness of Christ.
Elisabeth Elliot

an eXtremely good idea

Never stop learning: Your future depends, to a
very great extent, upon you. So keep learning and
keep growing personally *and* spiritually.

*Grow in grace and understanding of our
Master and Savior, Jesus Christ.
Glory to the Master, now and forever! Yes!*

2 Peter 3:18 MSG

*For You, O God, have tested us;
You have refined us as silver is refined.
You brought us into the net; You laid affliction
on our backs. You have caused men to ride over
our heads; we went through fire and through water;
but You brought us out to rich fulfillment.*

Psalm 66:10-12 NKJV

Dear Lord, help me to keep growing
spiritually and emotionally.
Let me live according to Your Word,
and let me grow in my faith
every day that I live.
Amen

17

Extreme Kindness

And be kind and compassionate to one another,
forgiving one another, just as God
also forgave you in Christ.

Ephesians 4:32 HCSB

indness is a choice. Sometimes, when we feel happy or generous, we find it easy to be kind. Other times, when we are discouraged or tired, we can scarcely summon the energy to utter a single kind word. But, God's commandment is clear: He intends that we make the conscious choice to treat others with kindness and respect, no matter our circumstances, no matter our emotions.

In the busyness and confusion of daily life, it is easy to lose focus, and it is easy to become frustrated. We are imperfect human beings struggling to manage our lives as best we can, but we often fall short. When we are distracted or disappointed, we may neglect to share a kind word or a kind deed. This oversight hurts others, but it hurts us most of all.

Today, slow yourself down and be alert for people who need your smile, your kind words, or your helping hand. Make kindness a centerpiece of your dealings with others. They will be blessed, and you will be too.

When you launch an act of kindness out
into the crosswinds of life,
it will blow kindness back to you.
Dennis Swanberg

The mark of a Christian is that he will walk
the second mile and turn the other cheek.
A wise man or woman gives the extra effort,
all for the glory of the Lord Jesus Christ.
John Maxwell

Do all the good you can. By all the means you can.
In all the ways you can. In all the places you can.
At all the times you can. To all the people you can.
As long as ever you can.
John Wesley

an eXtremely good idea

You can't just talk about it: In order to be a kind
person, you must do kind things. Thinking about
them isn't enough. So get busy! The day to start
being a more generous person is today!

*A kind person is doing himself a favor.
But a cruel person brings trouble upon himself.*

Proverbs 11:17 ICB

*Kind words are like honey—
sweet to the soul and healthy for the body.*

Proverbs 16:24 NLT

Dear Lord, help me see the needs of those
around me. Today, let me spread kind words
of thanksgiving and celebration in honor
of Your Son. Let forgiveness rule my heart,
and let my love for Christ be reflected
through the acts of kindness that
I extend to those who need the healing touch
of the Master's hand.

Amen

for Guys

18

Making the Most of Your Extreme Talents

*God has given gifts to each of you from
his great variety of spiritual gifts.
Manage them well so that God's generosity
can flow through you.*

1 Peter 4:10 NLT

All of us have special talents, and you are no exception. But your talent is no guarantee of success; it must be cultivated and nurtured; otherwise, it will go unused . . . and God's gift to you will be squandered.

In the 25th chapter of Matthew, Jesus tells the "Parable of the Talents." In it, He describes a master who leaves his servants with varying amounts of money (talents). When the master returns, some servants have put their money to work and earned more, to which the master responds, "Well done, good and faithful servant! You have been faithful with a few things; I will put you in charge of many things. Come and share your master's happiness!" (Matthew 25:21 NIV)

But the story does not end so happily for the foolish servant who was given a single talent but did nothing with it. For this man, the master has nothing but reproach: "You wicked, lazy servant . . . ." (Matthew 25:26 NIV) The message from Jesus is clear: We must use our talents, not waste them.

Your particular talent is an extremely valuable treasure on temporary loan from God. He intends that you use your talent to enrich the world *and* to enrich your own life. Value the gift that God has

given you, nourish it, make it grow, and share it with the world. Then, when you meet your Master face-to-face, you, too, will hear those wonderful words, "Well done, good and faithful servant! . . . Come and share your Master's happiness!"

> You are the only person on earth
> who can use your ability.
> *Zig Ziglar*

> Natural abilities are like natural plants;
> they need pruning by study.
> *Francis Bacon*

> In the great orchestra we call life,
> you have an instrument and a song,
> and you owe it to God to play them both sublimely.
> *Max Lucado*

an eXtremely good idea

Converting talent into skill requires work: Remember the old adage: "What we are is God's gift to us; what we become is our gift to God."

Do not neglect the gift that is in you.
1 Timothy 4:14 NKJV

*The man who had received the five talents brought
the other five. "Master," he said, "you entrusted me
with five talents. See, I have gained five more."
His master replied, "Well done, good and faithful
servant! You have been faithful with a few things;
I will put you in charge of many things.
Come and share your master's happiness."*
Matthew 25:20-21 NIV

Father, You have given me abilities to be
used for the glory of Your kingdom.
Give me the courage and the perseverance
to use those talents. Keep me mindful that
all my gifts come from You, Lord. Let me be
Your faithful, humble servant, and let me
give You all the glory and all the praise.
Amen

19

Setting an Extremely Good Example

*You should be an example to the believers in speech,
in conduct, in love, in faith, in purity.*

1 Timothy 4:12 HCSB

O kay, here's a question: What kind of example are you? Are you the kind of guy whose life serves as a powerful example of decency and morality? Are you a guy whose behavior serves as a positive role model for others? Are you the kind of guy whose actions, day in and day out, are based upon integrity, fidelity, and a love for the Lord? If so, you are not only blessed by God; you are also a powerful force for good in a world that desperately needs positive influences such as yours.

We live in a dangerous, temptation-filled world. That's why you encounter so many opportunities to stray from God's commandments. Resist those temptations! When you do, you'll earn God's blessings, and you'll serve as a positive role model for your family and friends.

Phillips Brooks advised, "Be such a man, and live such a life, that if every man were such as you, and every life a life like yours, this earth would be God's Paradise." And that's sound advice because our families and friends are watching . . . and so, for that matter, is God.

For one man who can introduce another to
Jesus Christ by the way he lives and by the atmosphere
of his life, there are a thousand who can only talk
jargon about him.

Oswald Chambers

We urgently need people who encourage and
inspire us to move toward God and away
from the world's enticing pleasures.

Jim Cymbala

Our walk counts far more than our talk, always!

George Mueller

There is nothing anybody else can do
that can stop God from using us . . .
We can turn everything into a testimony.

Corrie ten Boom

an eXtremely good idea

Living your life and shining your light . . . As
a Christian, the most important light you shine is
the light that your own life shines on the lives of
others. May your light shine brightly, righteously,
obediently, and eternally!

*Set an example of good works yourself,
with integrity and dignity in your teaching.*

Titus 2:7 HCSB

*You are the light that gives light to the world.
In the same way, you should be a light for
other people. Live so that they will see the good things
you do and will praise your Father in heaven.*

Matthew 5:14,16 NCV

Lord, make me a good example to
my family and friends. Let the things
that I say and do show everybody
what it means to be a good person
and a good Christian.
Amen

20

There's Work to Do!

*In all the work you are doing, work the best you can.
Work as if you were doing it for the Lord,
not for people.*

Colossians 3:23 NCV

Have you acquired the habit of doing first things first, or are you one of those guys who puts off important work until the last minute? The answer to this simple question will help determine how well you do your work *and* how much fun you have doing it.

God's Word teaches us the value of hard work. In his second letter to the Thessalonians, Paul warns, ". . . if any would not work, neither should he eat" (3:10 KJV). And the Book of Proverbs proclaims, "One who is slack in his work is brother to one who destroys" (18:9 NIV). In short, God has created a world in which diligence is rewarded and laziness is not. So, whatever it is that you choose to do, do it with commitment, excitement, and vigor. And remember this: Hard work is not simply a proven way to get ahead; it's also part of God's plan for you.

You have countless opportunities to accomplish great things for God—but you should not expect the work to be easy. So pray as if everything depended upon God, but work as if everything depended upon you. When you do, you should expect *very* big payoffs because when you and God become partners in your work, amazing things happen.

Thank God every morning when you get up
that you have something which must be done,
whether you like it or not. Work breeds
a hundred virtues that idleness never knows.

Charles Kingsley

The world does not consider labor a blessing,
therefore it flees and hates it, but the pious who
fear the Lord labor with a ready and cheerful heart,
for they know God's command, and they
acknowledge His calling.

Martin Luther

It may be that the day of judgment will dawn
tomorrow; in that case, we shall gladly stop working
for a better tomorrow. But not before.

Dietrich Bonhoeffer

an eXtremely good idea

**Wherever you happen to be, be the best you can
be**: Giving your best is habit-forming, so give your
best every time you go to work.

Whatever your hand finds to do,
do it with your might.
Ecclesiastes 9:10 NKJV

He who works his land will have abundant food,
but the one who chases fantasies
will have his fill of poverty.
Proverbs 28:19 NIV

Dear Lord, make my work pleasing to You.
Help me to sow the seeds of Your abundance
everywhere I go. Let me be passionate
in all my undertakings and
give me patience to wait for Your harvest.
Amen

Too Busy to Pray?

Then if my people who are called by my name
will humble themselves and pray and seek my face
and turn from their wicked ways,
I will hear from heaven and will forgive
their sins and heal their land.

2 Chronicles 7:14 NLT

Okay, from the looks of things, you're an *extremely* busy guy. And perhaps, because of your demanding schedule, you've neglected to pay sufficient attention to a particularly important part of your life: the spiritual part. If so, today is the day to change, and one way to make that change is simply to spend a little more time talking with God.

God is trying to get His message through to you. Are you listening?

Perhaps, on occasion, you may find yourself overwhelmed by the press of everyday life. Perhaps you may forget to slow yourself down long enough to talk with God. Instead of turning your thoughts and prayers to Him, you may rely upon your own resources. Instead of asking God for guidance, you may depend only upon your own limited wisdom. A far better course of action is this: simply stop what you're doing long enough to open your heart to God; then listen carefully for His directions.

In all things great and small, seek God's wisdom and His grace. He hears your prayers, and He will answer. All you must do is ask.

The more praying there is in the world,
the better the world will be,
the mightier the forces against evil everywhere.

E. M. Bounds

Prayer is not primarily my opportunity to
get from God what I want. Rather, prayer is a time
for me to know God better and to hear Him.

Henry Blackaby

I have heard some Christians say,
"I do not feel in a proper frame of mind to pray."
My brother, then pray until you do.

C. H. Spurgeon

an eXtremely good idea

Prayer strengthens your relationship with God…
so pray. D. L. Moody observed, "The Christian on
his knees sees more than the philosopher on tiptoe."
It's up to you to live—and pray—accordingly.

The intense prayer of the righteous is very powerful.
James 5:16 HCSB

*Whatever you ask for in prayer,
believe that you have received it,
and it will be yours.*
Mark 11:24 NIV

Dear Lord, make me a person whose
constant prayers are pleasing to You.
Let me come to You often with concerns
both great and small. I trust in the power
of prayer, Father, because prayer changes
things and it changes me. In the quiet
moments of the day, I will open my heart
to You. I know that You are with me always
and that You always hear my prayers.
So I will pray and be thankful.

Amen

22

Doing What's Right

*Are there those among you who are truly wise
and understanding? Then they should show it
by living right and doing good things
with a gentleness that comes from wisdom.*

James 3:13 NCV

Okay, answer this question honestly: Do you behave differently because of your relationship with Jesus, or do you behave in pretty much the same way that you would if you weren't a believer? Hopefully, the fact that you've invited Christ to reign over your heart means that you've made extreme changes in your thoughts and your actions.

Doing the right thing is not always easy, especially when you're tired or frustrated. But, doing the wrong thing almost always leads to trouble. And sometimes, it leads to big trouble.

> What is God looking for? He is looking for men and women whose hearts are completely His.
>
> *Charles Swindoll*

If you're determined to follow "the crowd," you may soon find yourself headed in the wrong direction. So here's some advice: Don't follow the crowd—follow Jesus. And keep following Him every day of your life.

for Guys

We pursue righteousness when we flee the things
that keep us from following the Lord Jesus.
These are the keys: flee, follow, and fight.

Franklin Graham

Have your heart right with Christ, and he will visit
you often, and so turn weekdays into Sundays,
meals into sacraments, homes into temples,
and earth into heaven.

C. H. Spurgeon

Christianity says we were created by a righteous
God to flourish and be exhilarated in a righteous
environment. God has "wired" us in such a way
that the more righteous we are,
the more we'll actually enjoy life.

Bill Hybels

an eXtremely good idea

**If you're not sure that it's the right thing to do,
don't do it!** And if you're not sure that it's the
truth, don't tell it.

For the LORD gives wisdom . . . .
He holds victory in store for the upright . . . .
Proverbs 2:6-7 NIV

But seek first his kingdom and his righteousness,
and all these things will be given to you as well.
Matthew 6:33 NIV

Dear Lord, this world has countless
temptations, distractions, interruptions,
and frustrations. When I allow my focus to
drift away from You and Your Word, I suffer.
But, when I turn my thoughts and my prayers
to You, Heavenly Father, You guide my path.
Let me discover the right thing to do—
and let me do it—this day and
every day that I live.
Amen

23

Extreme Perseverance

Thanks be to God! He gives us the victory through our Lord Jesus Christ. Therefore, my dear brothers, stand firm. Let nothing move you. Always give yourselves fully to the work of the Lord, because you know that your labor in the Lord is not in vain.

1 Corinthians 15:57-58 *NIV*

Are you one of those guys who doesn't give up easily, or are you quick to bail out when the going gets tough? If you've developed the unfortunate habit of giving up at the first sign of trouble, it's probably time for you to have a heart-to-heart talk with the guy you see every time you look in the mirror.

A well-lived life is like a marathon, not a sprint—it calls for preparation, determination, and lots of perseverance. As an example of perfect perseverance, you need look no further than your Savior, Jesus Christ.

Jesus finished what He began. Despite His suffering, despite the shame of the cross, Jesus was steadfast in His faithfulness to God. You, too, should remain faithful, especially when times are tough.

Are you facing a difficult situation? If so, remember this: whatever your problem, God can handle it. Your job is to keep persevering until He does.

Keep adding, keep walking, keep advancing;
do not stop, do not turn back,
do not turn from the straight road.
St. Augustine

That is the source of Jeremiah's living persistence,
his creative constancy. He was up before the sun,
listening to God's word. Rising early, he was quiet
and attentive before his Lord. Long before the yelling
started, the mocking, the complaining, there was
this centering, discovering, exploring time with God.
Eugene Peterson

Battles are won in the trenches, in the grit
and grime of courageous determination;
they are won day by day in the arena of life.
Charles Swindoll

an eXtremely good idea

The world encourages instant gratification, but God's work usually takes time. Remember the words of C. H. Spurgeon: "By perseverance, the snail reached the ark."

Finishing is better than starting.
Patience is better than pride.
Ecclesiastes 7:8 NLT

Let us not become weary in doing good,
for at the proper time we will reap
a harvest if we do not give up.
Galatians 6:9 NIV

Heavenly Father, sometimes, this life
is difficult indeed. Sometimes, I am fearful.
Sometimes, I cry tears of bitterness and
loss, but even then, You never leave my side.
Today, Lord, let me be a finisher of my faith.
Let me persevere—even if the day is difficult—
and let me follow Your Son Jesus
this day and forever.
Amen

24

Following in Those Extreme Footsteps

And what does the LORD require of you?
To act justly and to love mercy
and to walk humbly with your God.

Micah 6:8 NIV

Whom will you walk with today? Will you walk with people who worship the ways of the world? Or will you walk with the Son of God?

Jesus walks with you. Are you walking with Him? Hopefully, you will choose to walk with Him today and every day of your life.

Jesus has called upon believers of every generation (and that includes you) to follow in His footsteps. And God's Word promises that when you follow in Christ's footsteps, you will learn how to live freely and lightly (Matthew 11:28-30).

Are you worried about the day ahead? Be confident in God's power. He will never desert you. Are you concerned about the future? Be courageous and call upon God. He will protect you. Are you confused? Listen to the quiet voice of your Heavenly Father. He is not a God of confusion. Talk with God; listen to Him; follow His commandments . . . and walk with His Son—starting now.

Following in Those Extreme Footsteps

As a child of God, rest in the knowledge that
your Savior precedes you, and He will walk with you
through each experience of your life.

Henry Blackaby

If you'll flip from cover to cover, you'll notice that
it's overwhelmingly a book of stories—
tales of men and women who walked with God.

John Eldredge

An early walk and talk with the Lord will last all day.

Anonymous

an eXtremely good idea

Following Christ is a daily journey: When you
decide to walk in the footsteps of the Master, that
means that you're agreeing to be a disciple seven
days a week, not just on Sundays. Remember the
words of Vance Havner: "We must live in all kinds
of days, both high days and low days, in simple
dependence upon Christ as the branch on the vine.
This is the supreme experience."

Are you tired? Worn out? Burned out on religion?
Come to me. Get away with me and you'll recover
your life. I'll show you how to take a real rest.
Walk with me and work with me . . . watch how
I do it. Learn the unforced rhythms of grace.
I won't lay anything heavy or ill-fitting on you.
Keep company with me and you'll learn to live
freely and lightly.

Matthew 11:28-30 MSG

As you therefore have received Christ Jesus the Lord,
so walk in Him, having been firmly rooted and
now being built up in Him and established in
your faith, just as you were instructed,
and overflowing with gratitude.

Colossians 2:6-7 NASB

Dear Lord, each day I will walk with You.
As we walk together, I pray that
Your presence will be reflected in my life,
and that Your love will dwell within
my heart this day and every day.
Amen

25

No More Temper Tantrums!

*Patient people have great understanding,
but people with quick tempers
show their foolishness.*

Proverbs 14:29 NCV

Your temper is either your master or your servant. Either you control it, or it controls you. And the extent to which you allow anger to rule your life will determine, to a surprising degree, the quality of your relationships with others *and* your relationship with God.

Temper tantrums are usually unproductive, unattractive, unforgettable, and unnecessary. Perhaps that's why Proverbs 16:32 states that, "Controlling your temper is better than capturing a city" (NCV).

If you've allowed anger to become a regular visitor at your house, you should pray for wisdom, for patience, and for a heart that is so filled with forgiveness that it contains no room for bitterness. God will help you terminate your tantrums *if* you ask Him to—and that's a good thing because anger and peace cannot coexist in the same mind.

If you permit yourself to throw too many tantrums, you will forfeit—at least for now—the peace that might otherwise be yours through Christ. So obey God's Word by turning away from anger today and every day. You'll be glad you did, and so will your family and friends.

No More Temper Tantrums!

When you strike out in anger, you may miss
the other person, but you will always hit yourself.

Jim Gallery

Anger is the noise of the soul; the unseen irritant
of the heart; the relentless invader of silence.

Max Lucado

Is there somebody who's always getting your goat?
Talk to the Shepherd.

Anonymous

Bitterness and anger, usually over trivial things,
make havoc of homes, churches, and friendships.

Warren Wiersbe

an eXtremely good idea

No more temper tantrums! If you think you're
about to throw a tantrum, slow down, catch your
breath, and walk away if you must. It's better to
walk away than it is to strike out in anger.

A hot-tempered man stirs up dissension,
but a patient man calms a quarrel.
Proverbs 15:18 NIV

Don't become angry quickly,
because getting angry is foolish.
Ecclesiastes 7:9 NCV

Do not let the sun go down on your anger,
and do not give the devil an opportunity.
Ephesians 4:26-27 NASB

Lord, I can be so impatient, and I can
become so angry. Calm me down, Lord,
and give me the maturity and the wisdom
to be a patient, forgiving Christian.
Just as You have forgiven me, Father,
let me forgive others so that I can follow
the example of Your Son.
Amen

26

Your Extremely Bright Future

I can do everything through him that gives me strength.

Philippians 4:13 NIV

et's talk for a minute about the future . . . *your* future. How bright do you believe your future to be? Well, if you're a faithful believer, God has plans for you that are so bright that you'd better pack several pairs of sunglasses and a lifetime supply of sunblock!

The way that you think about your future will play a powerful role in determining how things turn out (it's called the "self-fulfilling prophecy," and it applies to everybody, including you). So here's another question: Are you expecting a terrific tomorrow, or are you dreading a terrible one? The answer to that question will have a powerful impact on the way tomorrow unfolds.

Today, as you live in the present and look to the future, remember that God has an amazing plan for you. Act—and believe—accordingly. And one more thing: don't forget the sunblock.

Life is a glorious opportunity.
Billy Graham

There is no limit to what God can make us—
if we are willing.
Oswald Chambers

God surrounds you with opportunity.
You and I are free in Jesus Christ, not to do whatever
we want, but to be all that God wants us to be.
Warren Wiersbe

Great opportunities often disguise themselves
in small tasks.
Rick Warren

an eXtremely good idea

Be a realistic optimist: Your attitude toward
the future will help create your future. So think
realistically about yourself and your situation while
making a conscious effort to focus on hopes, not
fears. When you do, you'll put the self-fulfilling
prophecy to work for you.

But we are hoping for something we do not have yet,
and we are waiting for it patiently.

Romans 8:25 NCV

For I know the thoughts that I think toward you,
says the LORD, thoughts of peace and not of evil,
to give you a future and a hope.
Then you will call upon Me and go and pray to Me,
and I will listen to you.

Jeremiah 29:11-12 NKJV

Lord, as I take the next steps on
my life's journey, let me take them with You.
Whatever this day may bring, I thank You
for the opportunity to live abundantly.
Let me lean upon You, Father—
and trust You—this day and forever.
Amen

How Bright
Is Your Light?

While ye have light, believe in the light,
that ye may be the children of light.

John 12:36 KJV

Are you living the triumphant life that God has promised? Or are you, instead, a spiritually shrinking violet? As you ponder that question, consider this: God does not intend that you live a life that is commonplace or mediocre. And He doesn't want you to hide your light "under a basket." Instead, He wants you to "Let your light so shine before men, that they may see your good works and glorify your Father in heaven" (Matthew 5:16 NKJV). In short, God wants you to live a triumphant life so that others might know precisely what it means to be a believer.

If you're a believer whose passion for Christ is evident for all to see, congratulations! But if you're plagued by the temptations and distractions of these troubled times—or if you've allowed the inevitable frustrations of everyday life to obscure the joy that is rightfully yours—it's time to recharge your spiritual batteries.

The Christian life should be a triumphal celebration, a daily exercise in thanksgiving and praise. Join that celebration today. And while you're at it, make sure that you let others know that you've joined.

> Virtue—even attempted virtue—brings light;
> indulgence brings fog.
>
> *C. S. Lewis*

Go. This is the command of our Lord. Where?
To the world, for it is the world that is on God's heart.
Out there are multitudes for whom Christ died.
And the minute you and I receive the light of
the gospel, we, at that moment, become responsible
for spreading that light to those who are still in
darkness. Granted, we cannot all go physically,
but we can go on our knees.

Kay Arthur

an eXtremely good idea

What if I'm uncomfortable talking about my faith? Remember: you're not giving the State of the Union Address—you're having a conversation. And besides, if you're not sure what to say, a good place to start is by asking questions, not making speeches.

*I have come as a light into the world,
that whoever believes in Me should not
abide in darkness.*

John 12:46 NKJV

*You are the light that gives light to the world . . . .
Live so that they will see the good things you do.
Live so that they will praise your Father in heaven.*

Matthew 5:14,16 ICB

Dear Lord, let my light shine brightly
for You. Let me be a good example for all
to see, and let me share love and kindness
with my family and friends,
today and every day.
Amen

28

Extreme Worship

But the hour is coming, and now is,
when the true worshipers will worship the Father
in spirit and truth; for the Father is seeking such
to worship Him. God is Spirit, and those who
worship Him must worship in spirit and truth.

John 4:23-24 NKJV

od has a wonderful plan for your life, and an important part of that plan includes worship. We should never deceive ourselves: every life is based upon some form of worship. The question is not whether we worship but what we worship.

Some of us choose to worship God. The result is an extreme harvest of joy, peace, and abundance. Others distance themselves from God by foolishly worshiping earthly possessions and personal gratification. To do so is a mistake of profound proportions.

Have you accepted the grace of God's only begotten Son? Then worship Him. Worship Him today and every day. Worship Him with sincerity and thanksgiving. Write His name on your heart and rest assured that He, too, has written your name on His.

It's our privilege to not only raise our hands in worship but also to combine the visible with the invisible in a rising stream of praise and adoration sent directly to our Father.

Shirley Dobson

It's the definition of worship: A hungry heart finding the Father's feast. A searching soul finding the Father's face. A wandering pilgrim spotting the Father's house. Finding God. Finding God seeking us. This is worship. This is a worshiper.

Max Lucado

an eXtremely good idea

Worship is not meant to be boxed up in a church building on Sunday morning. To the contrary, praise and worship should be woven into the very fabric of our lives. Do you take time each day to worship your Father in heaven, or do you wait until Sunday morning to praise Him for His blessings? The answer to this question will, in large part, determine the quality and direction of your life. So worship accordingly.

Worship the Lord your God and . . . serve Him only.
Matthew 4:10 HCSB

Worship the LORD with gladness. Come before him, singing with joy. Acknowledge that the LORD is God! He made us, and we are his. We are his people, the sheep of his pasture.
Psalm 100:2-3 NLT

Lord, when I slow down and take
the time to worship You, my soul is blessed.
Let me worship You every day of my life,
and let me discover the peace that can be
mine when I welcome You into my heart.
Amen

29

Praise,
Praise,
and More
Praise

Praise the LORD. Give thanks to the LORD,
for he is good; his love endures forever.

Psalm 106:1 NIV

The Bible makes it clear: it pays to praise God. But sometimes, we allow ourselves to become so preoccupied with the demands of everyday life that we forget to say "Thank You" to the Giver of all good gifts.

Worship and praise should be a part of everything we do. Otherwise, we quickly lose perspective as we fall prey to the demands of the moment.

Do you sincerely desire to be a worthy servant of the One who has given you eternal love and eternal life? Then praise Him for who He is and for what He has done for you. And don't just praise Him on Sunday morning. Praise Him all day long, every day, for as long as you live . . . and then for all eternity.

> Praise and thank God for who He is and for what He has done for you.
>
> *Billy Graham*

for Guys

Be not afraid of saying too much in
the praises of God;
all the danger is of saying too little.

Matthew Henry

Worship is an act which develops feelings for God,
not a feeling for God which is expressed in
an act of worship. When we obey the command
to praise God in worship, our deep, essential need to
be in relationship with God is nurtured.

Eugene Peterson

an eXtremely good idea

Praise Him! One of the main reasons you go to church is to praise God. But, you need not wait until Sunday rolls around to thank your Heavenly Father. Instead, you can praise Him many times each day by saying silent prayers that only He can hear.

But as for me, I will always have hope;
I will praise you more and more.

Psalm 71:14 NIV

Great is the LORD! He is most worthy of praise!
His greatness is beyond discovery!

Psalm 145:3 NLT

Heavenly Father, today and every day
I will praise You. I will praise You with
my thoughts, my prayers, my words,
and my deeds . . . now and forever.

Amen

30

Extreme
Trust

Blessed is he that trusts in the LORD.

Proverbs 16:20 NIV

The little sign behind the cash register is yellow and frayed, but it still conveys a humorous, straightforward message: "In God we trust . . . all others pay cash!" As believers in Christ, we are called upon to agree with the first half of the shopkeeper's message: "In God we trust . . . ."

Sometimes, because we are imperfect human beings who are afraid to trust God completely, we want absolute guarantees before we deliver the goods. But it doesn't work that way. Before we can expect God to work miracles in our lives, we must first trust Him with everything we have and everything we are. Then and only then will we begin to see the miraculous results of His endless love and His awesome power.

Do you aspire to do great things for God's kingdom? Then trust Him. Trust Him with every aspect of your life. Trust Him with your relationships. Trust Him with your finances. Follow His commandments and pray for His guidance. Then, wait patiently for God's revelations and for His blessings. In His own fashion and in His own time, God will bless you in ways that you never could have imagined.

Extreme Trust

Ten thousand enemies cannot stop a Christian,
cannot even slow him down, if he meets them in
an attitude of complete trust in God.

A. W. Tozer

The passwords that open the gates into the refuge
of God are the soul-wrenching words that flow
out of our hearts when we finally decide to trust God.

Bill Hybels

Trust in yourself and you are doomed to
disappointment; trust in money and you may
have it taken from you, but trust in God,
and you are never to be confounded
in time or eternity.

D. L. Moody

an eXtremely good idea

In God we trust? You bet! One of the most
important lessons that you can ever learn is to trust
God for everything—not some things, not most
things . . . everything!

*Jesus said, "Don't let your hearts be troubled.
Trust in God, and trust in me."*
John 14:1 NCV

*Trust in the LORD with all your heart;
do not depend on your own understanding.*
Proverbs 3:5 NLT

Dear Lord, I come to You today with hope
in my heart and praise on my lips.
I place my trust in You, Dear God, knowing
that with You as my Protector, I have nothing
to fear. I thank You, Father, for Your grace,
for Your Love, and for Your Son. Let me
follow in Christ's footsteps today and
every day that I live. And then,
when my work here is done,
let me live with You forever.
Amen

31

God's Extreme Love
(John 3:16)

*We know how much God loves us,
and we have put our trust in him. God is love,
and all who live in love live in God,
and God lives in them.*

1 John 4:16 NLT

God's love for you is bigger and better than you can imagine. In fact, God's love is far too big to comprehend (in this lifetime). But this much we know: God loves you so much that He sent His Son Jesus to come to this earth and to die for you. And, when you accepted Jesus into your heart, God gave you a gift that is more precious than gold: the gift of eternal life. Now, precisely because you are a wondrous creation treasured by God, a question presents itself: What will you do in response to God's love? Will you ignore it or embrace it? Will you return it or neglect it? The decision, of course, is yours and yours alone.

When you embrace God's love, you are forever changed. When you embrace God's love, you feel differently about yourself, your neighbors, and your world. When you embrace God's love, you share His message and you obey His commandments.

When you accept the Father's gift of grace, you are blessed here on earth *and* throughout all eternity. So do yourself a favor right now: accept God's love with open arms and welcome His Son Jesus into your heart. When you do, your life will be changed today, tomorrow, and forever.

God's Extreme Love (John 3:16)

If God had a refrigerator, your picture would be on it.
If he had a wallet, your photo would be in it.
He sends you flowers every spring
and a sunrise every morning.

Max Lucado

The hope we have in Jesus is the anchor for
the soul—something sure and steadfast,
preventing drifting or giving way,
lowered to the depth of God's love.

Franklin Graham

To lose us was too great a pain for God to bear,
and so he took it upon himself to rescue us.
The Son of God came "to give his life
as a ransom for many" (Matt. 20:28).

John Eldredge

an eXtremely good idea

Express yourself . . . If you sincerely love God, don't be too bashful to tell Him so. And while you're at it, don't be too bashful to tell other people about your feelings. If you love God, say so!

This is what real love is: It is not our love for God;
it is God's love for us in sending his Son
to be the way to take away our sins.

1 John 4:10 NCV

That is, in Christ, he chose us before the world
was made so that we would be his holy people—
people without blame before him. Because of his love,
God had already decided to make us his own children
through Jesus Christ. That was what he wanted
and what pleased him . . . .

Ephesians 1:4-5 NCV

Thank You, Lord, for Your love.
Your love is boundless, infinite, and eternal.
Today, let me pause and reflect upon
Your love for me, and let me share that love
with all those who cross my path. And,
as an expression of my love for You, Father,
let me share the saving message of
Your Son with a world in desperate need
of His peace.
Amen

More
Bible Verses
to Consider

Courage

Therefore, being always of
good courage . . .
we walk by faith, not by sight.
2 Corinthians 5:6-7 NASB

For God has not given us
a spirit of fear,
but of power and of love
and of a sound mind.
2 Timothy 1:7 NKJV

Be of good courage,
And He shall strengthen
your heart,
All you who hope in the LORD.
Psalm 31:24 NKJV

for Guys

I sought
the LORD, and he
answered me;
he delivered me
from all my fears.

-

Psalm 34:4 NIV

Hope

Without wavering,
let us hold tightly to the hope
we say we have, for God can be
trusted to keep his promise.
Hebrews 10:23 NLT

The LORD is good to those whose
hope is in him, to the one
who seeks him; it is good
to wait quietly for the salvation
of the LORD.
Lamentations 3:25-26 NIV

Happy is he . . . whose hope
is in the LORD his God.
Psalm 146:5 KJV

I find rest
in God; only
he gives me
hope.

Psalm 62:5 NCV

Discipline

For God did not give us
a spirit of timidity,
but a spirit of power,
of love and of self-discipline.
2 Timothy 1:7 NIV

He who heeds discipline shows
the way to life,
but whoever ignores correction
leads others astray.
Proverbs 10:17 NIV

My son, do not despise the Lord's
discipline and do not resent
his rebuke, because the Lord
disciplines those he loves,
as a father the son
he delights in.
Proverbs 3:11-12 NIV

The fear of the LORD is
the beginning of knowledge,
but fools despise wisdom
and discipline.

-

Proverbs 1:7 NIV

Faith

Thy faith hath made thee whole.
Matthew 9:22 KJV

I tell you the truth, if you have
faith and do not doubt . . .
you can say to this mountain
"Go and throw yourself
into the sea," and it will be done.
Matthew 21:21 NIV

The fundamental fact of existence
is that this trust in God,
this faith, is the firm foundation
under everything that makes
life worth living.
Hebrews 11:1 MSG

EVERYTHING IS POSSIBLE TO THE ONE WHO BELIEVES.

Mark 9:23 HCSB

Kindness

Thus has the Lord of hosts said,
"Dispense true justice and
practice kindness and compassion
each to his brother."
Zechariah 7:9 NASB

Be kindly affectionate to one
another with brotherly love,
in honor giving preference to one
another; not lagging in diligence,
fervent in spirit, serving the
Lord; rejoicing in hope, patient
in tribulation, continuing
steadfastly in prayer.
Romans 12:10-12 NKJV

I tell you the truth, whatever
you did for one of the least
of these brothers of mine,
you did for me.
Matthew 25:40 NIV

Be peaceable,
gentle,
showing every
consideration
for all men.

-

Titus 3:2 NASB

Wisdom

The LORD says, "I will make you wise
and show you where to go.
I will guide you and
watch over you."
Psalm 32:8 NCV

The wisdom that is from above is
first pure, then peaceable, gentle,
and easy to be entreated, full
of mercy and good fruits, without
partiality, and without hypocrisy.
James 3:17 KJV

Do not deceive yourselves.
If any one of you thinks he is wise
by the standards of this age,
he should become a "fool" so that
he may become wise. For the wisdom
of this world is foolishness
in God's sight.
1 Corinthians 3:18-19 NIV

for Guys

Teach me Your way, O Lord; I will walk in Your truth.

–

Psalm 86:11 NASB

Work

But one thing I do:
Forgetting what is behind and
straining toward what is ahead,
I press on toward the goal to win
the prize for which God has called
me heavenward in Christ Jesus.
Philippians 3:13-14 NIV

Then he said to his disciples,
"The harvest is plentiful
but the workers are few.
Ask the Lord of the harvest,
therefore, to send out workers
into his harvest field."
Matthew 9:37 NIV

for Guys

While it is daytime,
we must continue doing
the work of the One
who sent me.
Night is coming,
when no one can work.

-

John 9:4 NCV

Abundance

And God will generously provide all you need. Then you will always have everything you need and plenty left over to share with others.

2 Corinthians 9:8 NLT

His master replied, "Well done, good and faithful servant! You have been faithful with a few things; I will put you in charge of many things. Come and share your master's happiness!"

Matthew 25:21 NIV

My cup runs over. Surely goodness and mercy shall follow me all the days of my life; and I will dwell in the house of the LORD forever.

Psalm 23:5-6 NKJV

I have come that they may have life, and that they may have it more abundantly.

—

John 10:10 NKJV

Jesus

Therefore if any man be in Christ,
he is a new creature:
old things are passed away;
behold, all things are become new.

2 Corinthians 5:17 KJV

As the Father knoweth me,
even so know I the Father: and
I lay down my life for the sheep.

John 10:15 KJV

Jesus answered, "I am the way and
the truth and the life. No one
comes to the Father except through
me. If you really knew me,
you would know my Father as well.
From now on, you do know him and
have seen him."

John 14:6-7 NIV

Jesus Christ is the same yesterday, today, and forever.

-

Hebrews 13:8 HCSB

God's Love

Greater love has no one than this,
than to lay down one's life
for his friends.
John 15:13 NKJV

For God loved the world in this
way: He gave His only Son, so that
everyone who believes in Him will
not perish but have eternal life.
John 3:16 HCSB

Enter his gates with thanksgiving;
go into his courts with praise.
Give thanks to him and bless
his name. For the LORD is good.
His unfailing love continues
forever, and his faithfulness
continues to each generation.
Psalm 100:4-5 NLT

for Guys

But God demonstrates
his own love
for us in this:
While we were
still sinners,
Christ died for us.

-

Romans 5:8 NIV